BECOMING A LEADER
Workbook

Revised Edition

Myles Munroe

BECOMING A LEADER
Workbook

by Myles Munroe

Printed in the United States of America

Copyright © 1993 - Myles Munroe

Becoming A Leader Workbook - Revised Edition
ISBN 1-56229-412-1

Pneuma Life Publishing, Inc.
4451 Parliament Place
Lanham, MD 20706
301-577-4052
http://www.pneumalife.com

CONTENTS

INTRODUCTION

I trust that if you are now reading this, you are serious about becoming a leader. That is what this workbook is all about. The questions and assignments given here are designed to help you activate the leadership potential within you.

Each chapter begins with a passage of Scripture that enhances the principles learned in that chapter. It should be read before any study is done.

The next step is the questions. Most are directly from the text of "Becoming A Leader" by Myles Munroe. There is a combination of question and answer, true or false, multiple choice and fill in the blank questions to help you receive the full benefit of the text. There are also personal questions that you may have to work a little harder to find the answer to. Please make that extra effort. Doing so will help you internalize leadership principles and give you the tools necessary to change your life!

Following the questions is the "Assignment" section. This is a section that asks questions and gives you projects that are more in depth. Through these projects, you will have the opportunity to put into practice what you are learning. And, you will be able to see your progress. To successfully complete this section, you will need a small notebook. In it you will record your answers and your thoughts as you work through each chapter. When you have completed this workbook, it will be good to go back through your notebook and see how much God has taught you.

For those of you leading a class or Bible Study, "Group Study" ideas have been included. These ideas will help you stimulate good discussion and involve all members of your class.

Next, is the "Memory Verse." This has been taken out of the Scripture passage in each chapter. For maximum benefit, it should be memorized before moving on to the next chapter. One idea to help you do this is, write it out on a 3x5 card and tape it to your bathroom mirror. Every morning and every evening meditate on the verse.

May God bless you as you begin your study on "Becoming A Leader!"

CHAPTER 1

UNDERSTANDING LEADERSHIP

Scripture Passage: John 14:23-31

In this chapter you will learn:

1. A working definition of leadership
2. Who is destined for leadership
3. God's intention for his people regarding leadership

1. Leadership is: _____

   _____

   _____

   _____

   _____

   _____

2. Based on this definition, list your personal leadership experiences. For example, in parenthood, in friendships, etc. List as many as you can think of. _____

   _____

   _____

   _____

   _____

   _____

3. Leadership has very little to do with _____, and is fundamentally a matter of _____.

As you complete this study, it is important to note that character development is the essence of becoming a leader. Character separates the immature from the mature.

4. List the philosophical concept of leadership that has produced the historical, global concept that the masses are destined to be ruled by a privileged few. _____

   _____

   _____

   _____

   _____

5. According to the text, is this correct? _____

6. Developing _____ and _____ is the way leaders are made.

7. The text gives some examples of unlikely leaders in the Bible. List the leaders and their significant accomplishment.

   a. _____
   b. _____
   c. _____
   d. _____

8. Now list the obstacles that each of these men had to overcome.
   a. _____
   b. _____
   c. _____
   d. _____

9. Make your own list of people in history or people you know who overcame obstacles in their lives to become great leaders. _____

   _____

   _____

   _____

10. According to the text, is there a leader within you? _____

11. How do we need to see ourselves?
    a. In leadership
    b. As our Creator sees us
    c. Both

12. When does the leader within you become alive? _____

    _____

    _____

    _____

    _____

    _____

13. List three dreams you have for your life and list on another sheet of paper ten steps to accomplish those dreams.

    1. _____

    2. _____

    3. _____

14. How did God create us? _____

    _____

    _____

    _____

15. Deeply embedded in the nature of man are the_____
    and _____.

16. List the five principles that are fundamental to our very nature and fulfillment:

    a. _____

    b. _____

    c. _____

    d. _____

    e. _____

17. To whom were we designed to be subjected?
    a. The government
    b. Our pastor
    c. The Holy Spirit

18. What led to the need for external government? _____
    _____
    _____
    _____

19. What is God's plan for the human race? _____
    _____
    _____
    _____

20. What energy supply do we need in order to perform our purpose?
    _____
    _____
    _____

"To a leader, life is a career"

Assignment:

As you complete this section, consider your personal definition of leadership. Is it different from the principles given here? If so, how? What needs to be changed in the following: How you see yourself? How you see others? The level of personal responsibility you take in your life? And, perhaps most importantly, address whether or not you believe God has called you to be a leader?

Take some time in the next few days to prayerfully answer these questions. Record those answers in a small notebook and keep it with you as you continue to study this workbook.

Group Study:

Discuss questions 2 and 9 as a group. Use "Assignment" section as out of class work. Small group exercise: Come up with a definition for character. What are some important components of character?

Memory Verse:

John 14:26 "But the Counselor, the Holy Spirit, whom the Father will send in my name, will teach you all things and will remind you of everything I have said to you."

CHAPTER 2

WHAT IS LEADERSHIP?

Scripture: John 13:3-17

In this chapter you will learn:

1. The difference between "leader" and "leadership"
2. A working definition of leadership
3. The components of leadership

1. Is there a difference between "leadership" and "the leader"? _____
    _____
    _____

2. The leader is the _____, _____ and the
    _____ assuming the position.

3. Leadership is the _____ of the designated _____ and the
    _____ of the _____ involved in the position.

4. In your own words, what is the difference between "the leader" and
    "leadership?" _____
    _____
    _____
    _____
    _____
    _____
    _____

5. Does title and position guarantee performance and productivity?

    _____

    _____

6. Have you ever known a leader who did not provide leadership?

    _____

    _____

7. Out of the following list, circle the words that describe leadership:

    influence   inspiration   visibility
    power   mobilize   authority
    motivation   confidence   momentum

8. Leadership organizes and coordinates:
    a. resources
    b. energies
    c. relationships
    d. all of the above

9. Give two examples of "resources."
    1. _____
    2. _____

10. Why is organizing relationships important in leadership?_____

    _____

    _____

    _____

    _____

    _____

11. Leadership is impossible without:
    a. a guiding vision
    b. purpose
    c. both

12. What do these two things generate? _____
    _____
    _____
    _____

13. From what three things does leadership derive its power?
    a. _____
    b. _____
    c. _____

14. "Where there is no _____ the people cast off _____."
                                                    Proverbs 29:18

15. The two components of leadership are:
    a. _____
    b. _____

16. Which component must you have more of in order to experience effective leadership?
    a. vision and values
    b. inspiration and motivation
    c. they must be in balance

17. The purest form of leadership is: _____
    _____
    _____
    _____
    _____

18. Inspiration is the opposite of _____ and is absence of
    _____.

19. In your own words, why is inspiration more effective than intimidation?
    _____
    _____
    _____
    _____

"The discovery of self is the birth of leadership."

Assignment:

Refer back to question 13. In your notebook, write a definition of: a. values b. deep convictions and c. correct principles.

Why do you think these three things are important in leadership? Do you believe that they provide the power of leadership as the author states? If so, why? Record your answers in your notebook.

Group Ideas:

Discuss questions 4, 9, and 19 as a group. Small group work: Discuss why the discovery of self is the birth of leadership. What does the author mean by that?

Memory Verse:

John 13:15 "I have set you an example that you should do as I have done for you."

CHAPTER 3

WHAT IS A LEADER?

Scripture: Romans 15:1-6

In this chapter you will learn:

1. The definition of a leader
2. Characteristics of leaders
3. The difference between a leader and a manager

1. True or False. Many people die without ever knowing who they really were.

2. You were _____ to lead, but you must _____ a leader.

3. A leader is:
   a. one who guides by influence
   b. one who directs by going before or along with
   c. both

4. In your own words, what is the difference between subordinates and followers? _____
   _____
   _____
   _____
   _____
   _____
   _____

5.   True or False. A leader should feel threatened if one of his followers becomes a leader himself.

6.   What do you think it means for a leader to lead himself? _____

     _____

     _____

     _____

     _____

     _____

     _____

7.   List the five characteristics common to leadership:
     a. _____
     b. _____
     c. _____
     d. _____
     e. _____

8.   Discovering personal purpose for your life is finding _____ and _____ for living.

9.   According to the author, purpose means the reason for our creation. What do you think God's reason for your creation was? (Be as specific as you can.) _____

     _____

     _____

     _____

     _____

     _____

10. In your own words, why is a life without purpose a study in chaos and an exercise in frustration? _____

     _____

     _____

     _____

     _____

     _____

11. Purpose provides the fuel for:
    a. perseverance
    b. persistence
    c. passion
    d. all of the above

12. Integrity involves _____, _____ and
    _____.

13. True or False. A leader needs to have had experience as a follower.

14. Why do you think this is? _____
    _____
    _____
    _____

15. Trust is the one quality that cannot be _____; it must be
    _____.

16. Trust is a product of _____ and _____.

17. At this time in your life, what are some things you can do to earn the trust
    of others? _____
    _____
    _____
    _____
    _____
    _____

18. A leader is willing to take _____, step out in _____,
    _____ new things and _____ convention.

19. If these qualities do not come naturally to you, is it possible to change?
    _____
    _____
    _____
    _____

20. According to the text, what gives you the ability to face the unknown?

    _____
    _____
    _____
    _____

21. True or False. A leader has confidence in someone else's value system.

22. In order to know yourself, what must you separate? _____

    _____
    _____

23. Is it more important for leaders to prove themselves or express themselves?

    _____
    _____

24. Why do you think full expression in this context would bring glory to God?

    _____
    _____
    _____
    _____

25. List the four types of people in this world:
    a. _____
    b. _____
    c. _____
    d. _____

26. Leaders fall into which category? _____

    _____

27. Leaders _____ the context, managers _____ to it.

28. True or False. A leader can be trusted with very much or very little.

29.   What does a leader NOT attempt to do? _____

_____

_____

_____

_____

30.   True or False. It is important that everyone in the Body of Christ have the same personality.

"If we knew the source of public judgments, we would
cease to strive for them." - Marcus Aurelius

"The basic function of the leader is to provide an environment that fosters mutual respect and builds a complementary, cohesive team, where each unique strength is made productive and each weakness is made irrelevant."

Assignment:

In your notebook, at the top of each of the next five pages, write one of the following questions:
1. What is my purpose?
2. What is my passion?
3. At what level of integrity do I live my life?
4. How trustworthy am I?
5. How curious and daring am I?

   Take some time right now to evaluate yourself in each of the five areas. As you work through this book, turn back to these questions periodically and re-evaluate yourself. When you reach the end of the study, you will be able to chart your growth and understanding. If you have any insight into any of these areas, jot those down as well.

Group Study:

Discuss questions 4, 6, 10, 17, and 24 as a group. In small groups, make a list of reasons why purpose is so important in the life of a leader.

Memory Verse:

Romans 15:5 "May the God who gives endurance and encouragement give you a spirit of unity among yourselves as you follow Christ Jesus."

CHAPTER 4

THE PURPOSE FOR LEADERSHIP

Scripture: Matthew 16:24-27

In this chapter you will learn:

1. The definition of success
2. The objective of following
3. The real purpose of leadership

1. True success is:
   a. lots of followers
   b. the fulfillment of the original purpose
   c. finishing what you started

2. Effectiveness is: _____
   _____
   _____
   _____
   _____
   _____
   _____

3. It is possible to zealously, efficiently, successfully and sincerely do an excellent job on the _____ thing and therefore _____.

4. You can be busy but not _____, active but not _____.

5. The "right thing" equals _____.

6. What should you know before you assume responsibility for a task?
   a. its purpose
   b. how it's to be done
   c. who will help you

7. To understand the purpose for leadership, what must we discover?

   _____

   _____

   _____

   _____

   _____

8. Whatever God calls for, He _____ for.

9. Therefore, if we are all called to leadership, do we all have the capacity to lead? _____

   _____

10. What happened that resulted in man's loss of his position of dominance in the world? _____

    _____

    _____

    _____

    _____

    _____

11. True or False. The maintenance of followers is the goal of leadership.

12. True leadership leads followers into _____ themselves and inspires them to _____ themselves.

13. The ultimate goal of leadership is:
    a. numbers
    b. independence
    c. dependence

14. List the three phases of life experience:
    a. _____
    b. _____
    c. _____

15. List one example for each of these phases. _____
    _____
    _____
    _____
    _____
    _____
    _____
    _____
    _____
    _____

16. When can you fully contribute to the lives of others? _____
    _____
    _____
    _____
    _____

17. The purpose for leadership is: _____
    _____
    _____
    _____
    _____

18. Give some examples of leaders you know of who are living out this principle of leadership. _____
    _____
    _____
    _____
    _____
    _____
    _____

19. What was the ultimate measure of Jesus' success as a leader?
    a. He left
    b. He died
    c. He rose again
    d. all of the above

20. Success without a _____ is failure.

21. In your own words, why is this principle true? _____
    _____
    _____
    _____
    _____
    _____
    _____
    _____

"To be yourself and become your potential is the essence of life."

Assignment:

Read Eph. 4:10-14. In your notebook, list the offices of leadership that God established in the Body of Christ. What is their function? What are the four reasons for doing this? What is the final result?

In your own life, how are you working to see God's people become mature? How CAN you work to see God's people mature?

In whatever capacity of leadership you are now in, are you confident enough to lead others into independence?

Group Study:

Discuss examples of doing the wrong thing well. Talk about why this is ineffective.

Discuss the difference between being busy and being effective.

In small groups, discuss question 21.

Memory Verse:

Matthew 16:24 "If anyone would come after me, he must deny himself and take up his cross and follow me."

CHAPTER 5

ARE YOU LEADERSHIP MATERIAL?

Scripture: II Thessalonians 3:6-13

In this chapter you will learn:
The proper motivation for leadership.

"The greatest display of leadership is service."

1. Leadership is the discovery and marriage of:
    a. purpose
    b. personality
    c. potential
    d. all of the above

2. List three questions you must ask yourself to assess your personal motivation for leadership. _____
    _____
    _____
    _____
    _____
    _____
    _____

3. If you want to make a difference in this world you must:
    a. count the cost
    b. make the loudest noise
    c. have the largest following

4.   Preparation includes a building of _____.

5.   True or False. There is a hidden leader in all of us.

6.   True or False. We must squash the desire to be a leader in order to do God's will.

7.   To be an effective leader you must be _____.

8.   From where does all leadership get its essence and context?_____

    _____

    _____

    _____

    _____

    _____

9.   What ambitions need to be guarded against? _____

    _____

    _____

    _____

    _____

    _____

10. Give two of your own examples of inappropriate ambition._____

    _____

    _____

    _____

    _____

    _____

    _____

    _____

    _____

11. True or False. A desire to be great is always sinful.

12. When is this ambition not sinful? _____

_____

_____

_____

_____

13. True or False. If your heart motivation is wrong, you don't have to worry because no one will ever know.

14. The principle of true leadership is: _____

_____

_____

_____

_____

_____

15. Selfish ambition will end in:
    a. obscurity
    b. success
    c. self-destruction

16. Can you name leaders who experienced this? _____

_____

_____

_____

_____

_____

_____

17. Ambition correctly channeled promotes what? _____

_____

_____

_____

_____

_____

_____

18. What does true, effective leadership demand? _____
_____
_____
_____
_____
_____

19. Name leaders that you know of who made this sacrifice. _____
_____
_____
_____
_____
_____
_____
_____

Assignment:

Take the personal motivation test found in question two. Record your answers. If your motivation is self-serving rather than selfless, what can you do to change that? Remember, only you will see your answers, so be completely honest.

Group Study:

Discuss questions 16 and 19 as a group. In small groups, determine how the wrong heart motivation will evidence itself.

Memory Verse:

II Thessalonians 3:9 "We did this, not because we do not have the right to such help, but in order to make ourselves a model for you to follow."

CHAPTER 6

THE PRINCIPLE KEY TO TRUE LEADERSHIP

Scripture: Hebrews 12:1-13

In this chapter you will learn:
1. The responses to the use of power
2. The key to leadership
3. The natural and spiritual characteristics of leadership

1. List the three highly predictable responses to the use of power:
    a. _____
    b. _____
    c. _____

2. What do people generally do when pushed by someone?_____
    _____
    _____
    _____
    _____

3. What do people generally do when faced with a relationship characterized by continual conflict? _____
    _____
    _____
    _____
    _____

4.   In an attempt to avoid conflict and risk, submissive subordinates do
     what? _____

     _____

     _____

     _____

5.   From your own experience, give an example of each of these responses.

     _____

     _____

     _____

     _____

6.   List three negative styles of leadership. _____

     _____

     _____

     _____

     _____

7.   True or False. A good leader will force his followers to do the work
     necessary for success.

8.   The only power a leader truly has is:
     a. the power of inspiration
     b. the power of authority
     c. the power of organization

**"Leadership is not dominating others,
rather it is serving and meeting needs."**

9.   The quality of inspiration is:
     a. the capacity to cause others to internalize a quality decision
     b. to help others discover themselves, their purpose and abilities
     c. to help others maximize their potential
     d. all of the above

10. What is the source of true inspiration? _____
     _____

11. What does a true leader live to do?
     a. to organize activities
     b. to fully express and be oneself
     c. to lead people

12. What is one thing that happens when you discover yourself? _____
     _____
     _____
     _____

13. How many methods are there of discovering your self-worth? _____
     _____
     _____
     _____

14. What must you do to discover yourself? _____
     _____
     _____
     _____

15. True or False. Leadership comes to those who campaign for it.

16. Faithfulness in the _____ things is the qualification for
     promotion to _____ things.

17. The person most likely to be successful is the one who does what?
     _____
     _____
     _____

18. True or False. We are to put aside our natural abilities in order to serve
     God His way.

19. True leadership does not come as a result of an _____ to lead or be great, but a deep desire to _____ others.

20. Natural leadership qualities and characteristics can only experience their highest effectiveness when:
    a. they are submitted to God
    b. employed by the purposes of God
    c. both

21. When natural qualities are exercised in leadership without being submitted to spiritual authority, what happens? _____

    _____

    _____

    _____

    _____

    _____

"Genuine leadership is a marriage of the natural and spiritual qualities producing a well integrated character."

22. List three comparisons between "natural" and "spiritual" leadership as listed in the book. _____

    _____

    _____

    _____

    _____

    _____

    _____

23. True or False. As a man knows God, he also learns and understands the nature of mankind.

24. Why does a true leader stand independent of circumstances and environmental influences? _____

    _____

"Inspiration is the key to aspiration."

Assignment:

Are there any aspects of your natural personality that you feel are not necessarily spiritual? If so, think about how they can be used to the glory of God. Do you believe that your natural abilities are given to you by God?

In your private devotions, begin asking God to give you a picture of how He can use your natural abilities in combination with spiritual principles you learn from His Word to make you into a truly effective leader for Him. Praise Him for doing this.

Group Study:

Discuss question 5 as a group. Discuss the importance of inspiration and how it can be used in leadership. In small groups, discuss natural characteristics. How they can be used for God and how our weaknesses can be turned into strengths.

Memory Verse:

Hebrews 12:2 "Let us fix our eyes on Jesus, the author and perfecter of our faith, who for the joy set before him endured the cross, scorning its shame, and sat down at the right hand of the throne of God."

CHAPTER 7

TAPPING YOUR
LEADERSHIP POTENTIAL PART I

Scripture: James 1:2-8

In this chapter you will learn:

A test for leadership potential.

"Great leaders are ordinary people who did extraordinary things because circumstances made demands on their potential."

1. An innovator:
    a. does things other people haven't done or won't do
    b. does things in advance of other people
    c. makes new things
    d. all of the above

2. True or False. Great leaders in history were people who had talents and advantages that we don't have.

3. We are our own _____.

In this chapter you will be able to assess your leadership potential and the extent of refinement you may need in order to further develop your skills for effective leadership. These qualities are introduced in this workbook for the purpose of self-evaluation. Please be as honest and as thorough as possible in answering the following questions.

INDEPENDENT DECISION MAKING

4. Do you think independently? _____
    _____
    _____

5. Leaders _____ from others, but they are not _____
    by others.

6. List a passage of scripture where Jesus displayed this quality.
    _____
    _____
    _____

GOVERN YOURSELF

7. Do you retain control of yourself when things go wrong? _____
    _____

8. If weather shapes mountains, what shapes a leader?
    a. education
    b. problems
    c. experience
    d. all of the above

9. Do you impose strict discipline and high standards on yourself?
    _____

ABILITY TO CONTROL ANGER

10. Do you manage your emotions? _____

11. True or False. Only the leaders with the largest following are targets
    of criticism.

12. "But a _____ man is one who controls his
    _____."

INDEPENDENT THINKER

13. Can you make decisions independently, without relying on other people's opinions? _____

_____

14. True or False. To think independently, you must ignore the contribution of others.

15. A good leader will _____ the value of _____ input.

CONQUER YOURSELF

16. Have you ever broken yourself of a bad habit? _____

_____

_____

17. What does it take to break a bad habit?
    a. personal integrity and desire
    b. a plan
    c. will-power

CREATIVELY HANDLE DISAPPOINTMENTS

18. How do you handle disappointment? _____

_____

_____

_____

_____

_____

19. True leaders see disappointments as _____ to maximize their _____ and they learn from _____.

20. Give three examples from Scripture of leaders creatively handling disappointment. _____

    _____

    _____

    _____

    _____

    _____

21. Can you keep yourself calm in a crisis? _____

    _____

INSPIRES CONFIDENCE

22. Do you readily secure the cooperation and win the respect and confidence of others? _____

    _____

    _____

    _____

23. What are the three things people can see in order to have confidence in you?

    a _____

    b. _____

    c. _____

RELIABLE

24. Are you entrusted with handling difficult and delicate situations?

    _____

    _____

25. Name the Biblical example of this quality. _____

    _____

    _____

    _____

    _____

    _____

CORRECTION

26. Do you possess the ability to secure discipline without having to resort to a show of authority? _____
_____

27. What is the sign that you are leading by inspiration? _____
_____
_____
_____

MOBILIZATION

28. Can you induce people to happily do some legitimate thing that they would not normally do? _____

29. The key to mobilization is _____.

CONCILIATOR

30. Are you considered a peace maker–one who finds it easier to keep the peace than to make peace where it has been shattered? _____
_____
_____

31. Conciliation is: _____
_____
_____
_____
_____
_____

ANTAGONISM

32. Can you accept opposition to your view point or decision without considering it a personal affront and reacting accordingly? _____
_____

RELATIONSHIPS

33. Do people seek your company? _____

34. Write out Proverbs 18:19. _____
_____
_____
_____

UNCONDITIONAL ACCEPTANCE OF OTHERS

35. Are you really interested in people–people of all types and all races?
_____

36. You cannot really _____ people if you don't
_____ them.

SELF-CONFIDENT

37. Are you intimidated by others and compare yourself with the abilities
and accomplishments of others? _____
_____
_____

38. If you follow God, where will He take you? _____
_____
_____

APPROACHABLE

39. Do your subordinates appear at ease in your presence? _____
_____
_____
_____
_____

EGO STRENGTH

40.   Are you unduly dependent on the praise and approval of others?

_____

_____

CENTERED

41.   Do you possess a strong and steady will? _____

_____

42.   Who is the negative example of this quality named here? _____

_____

_____

Assignment:

The next chapter is a continuation of these qualities, but let's pause here and look over your self-evaluation. In your notebook, record first a list of your strengths. Give a brief description of how that quality is manifested in your life. Next, list your weaknesses in the same way.

Group Study:

Encourage the group to take as much time as necessary between now and your next meeting to answer these questions as thoroughly as possible. For group discussion, give the story of the woman at the well in your own words. Discuss how it illustrates the quality of "Unconditional Acceptance of Others" and practical ways it applies to leadership.

Memory Verse:

James 1:5 "If any of you lacks wisdom, he should ask God, who gives generously to all without finding fault, and it will be given to him."

CHAPTER 7

TAPPING YOUR LEADERSHIP POTENTIAL PART II

Scripture: James 1:19-27

In this chapter you will learn:

More qualities of leadership.

Please continue with your personal evaluation of these qualities.

FORGIVING

1.   Do you nurse resentments or do you readily forgive injuries done to you? Why? _____
_____

2.   What are some reasons why Joseph would have an excuse to nurse resentment? _____
_____
_____
_____

3.   True or False. Behavior and potential are the same thing.

PURPOSEFUL

4. Do you have a driving, guiding vision that grips your soul with passion? What is your vision? _____

   _____

   _____

ENCOURAGING

5. Are you reasonably optimistic? How could you become more optimistic?

   _____

6. Nothing is impossible if you believe in who? _____

   _____

"When you don't know what else to do, encourage."

RESPONSIBILITY

7. Do you welcome responsibility? _____

   _____

8. True or False. As a leader, it isn't important to be responsible for menial tasks.

9. When people fail, how does a good leader treat them? _____

   _____

   _____

10. True or False. As a leader, you only need to be concerned with how to handle the failure of others.

"As in every seed there is a forest, so in every follower there is a leader."

Assignment:

Add the qualities in this chapter to the appropriate strength or weakness list in your notebook. Take your list of weaknesses and go back through the text. Look for ways the author gives for how to turn those weakness into strengths.

Group Study:

Continue with this chapter in the same way in which you completed the last chapter. Discuss the story of Joseph and how it illustrates the quality of "forgiveness." Discuss the importance of forgiveness in the life of a leader.

Memory Verse:

James 1:25 "But the man who looks intently into the perfect law that gives freedom and continues to do this–he will be blessed in what he does."

CHAPTER 8

QUALIFICATIONS FOR LEADERSHIP

Scripture: II Peter 1:3-11

In this chapter you will learn:

Essential qualities of character.

"The quality of your character is the measure of your leadership effectiveness."

1. Character, in its truest form, is the perfect balance of _____, _____ and _____.

2. True or False. It is best if a leader keeps his personal and professional lives completely separated.

3. What is the fuel of leadership?
    a. rules
    b. trust
    c. organization
    d. all of the above

4. Leaders are not _____, but are created by _____.

5. What does it take to become the leader you have the potential to become?

   _____

   _____

   _____

   _____

6. True or False. Each generation must decide which principles of leadership are right for them.

7. Name the passage of Scripture from which the qualifications of leadership are taken. _____

   _____

COMMITMENT TO INTEGRITY

8. Where will a man or woman's faithfulness be proven? _____

   _____

9. Being a _____ leader isn't enough, you must also be

   _____.

MORAL AND ETHICAL QUALIFICATIONS

10. True or False. If a leader is living right he will not experience temptations.

11. How can a leader best defend himself against temptation? _____

    _____

    _____

12. If a leader cannot control his passions, what should he do? _____

    _____

    _____

13. Be _____ to hear, _____ to speak, and slow to get _____.

TEMPERAMENT QUALIFICATIONS

14. A leader must have a proper _____ of himself in _____
    _____.

15. If your body is a place of residence for Jesus Christ, what should you not
    put into it? _____
    _____

16. Self-control is learning how to say:
    a. No
    b. maybe
    c. later

17. A leader must not be easily _____ by the behavior
    and offenses of others.

18. Meekness is:
    a. self-abasement
    b. controlled power
    c. humility

19. A leader must _____ and be _____
    with power.

THE QUALITY OF MATURITY

20. What is maturity? _____
    _____
    _____
    _____

21. What is maturity the product of?
    a. security
    b. time
    c. background
    d. all of the above

22. A leader should be willing to gain experience over _____ and understand that he has to _____ for the _____ of others.

INTELLECTUAL QUALIFICATIONS

23. True leaders are constantly reaching for more what?
    a. responsibility
    b. followers
    c. knowledge

24. In order to _____, you must be able to _____.

25. True or False. You can only learn in a classroom or at church.

26. List four things that those who are aspiring to become leaders do.
    1. _____
    2. _____
    3. _____
    4. _____

27. True leaders _____ their own learning.

FAMILY AND DOMESTIC QUALIFICATIONS

28. What will not be sacrificed for anything?
    a. position
    b. family
    c. the people

29. A leader must be found faithful in _____.

30. What two things are leaders to be good stewards of?
    a. _____
    b. _____

31. Management is the coordination of _____,
_____ and _____ toward a worthy
objective.

Assignment:

List the six qualifications for leadership in your notebook. Write your own definition for each. Identify those which are already part of your character and those which are more difficult for you to do. List a few ways you can be more conscience of incorporating all six of these qualifications into your daily life.

Choose one qualification to work on this week. Record your progress.

Group Study:

Read I Timothy 3:1-7 and decide which qualification each requirement falls under. In small groups, name some warnings that would indicate a person is not living up to these qualifications in his leadership and in his life.

Memory Verse:

II Peter 1:8 "For if you possess these qualities in increasing measure, they will keep you from being ineffective and unproductive in your knowledge of our Lord Jesus Christ."

CHAPTER 9

ESSENTIAL QUALITIES
OF LEADERSHIP

Scripture: Isaiah 42:5-9

In this chapter you will learn:

1.　　Characteristics of leadership
2.　　How to incorporate them into your own life

DISCIPLINE

1.　Discipline requires _____.

2.　True or False. It is better to discipline yourself than to let someone else do it for you.

3.　Who has earned the right to discipline others? _____
　　_____
　　_____
　　_____
　　_____

VISION

4.　What is a "seer?"_____
　　_____
　　_____

5. You must have foresight and _____.

6. True or False. A visionary will go with the flow just to get things done.

7. Without a vision, people _____.

8. A task without a vision is what? _____
    _____
    _____

9. What two things is vision the source of?
    a. _____
    b. _____

10. Write your own definition of vision. _____
    _____
    _____
    _____
    _____
    _____
    _____
    _____

COMMON SENSE

11. What is another word for common sense? _____
    _____

12. Wisdom is: _____
    _____
    _____
    _____
    _____
    _____
    _____
    _____

13. List three things that wisdom consists of:
    a. _____
    b. _____
    c. _____

14. Wisdom should not be confused with _____.

15. Wisdom comes from:
    a. study
    b. experience
    c. above

DECISIVENESS

16. Decisiveness is simply making a _____.

17. Let your _____ be yes and your _____ be no.

FORTITUDE

18. Fortitude means the same as:
    a. humility
    b. courageous
    c. perseverance

19. _____ fortitude will help you combat temptation.

20. With what will courage allow you to face difficulty?_____
    _____
    _____
    _____

21. True or False. Courage is the absence of fear.

22. From where comes our strength?
    a. perseverance
    b. acceptance
    c. joy

HUMILITY

23. Humility is:
    a. the ability to be yourself
    b. self-abasement
    c. meekness

24. True leaders are _____ humble.

25. In your own words, where does this humility come from?_____
    _____
    _____
    _____

26. True or False. True leaders should be able to give honor and recognition to others without hesitation.

27. Humility is the result of:
    a. practice
    b. God's love and mercy in your life
    c. hard work
    d. all of the above

28. True or False. A leader does not have to do the jobs nobody else wants. He can appoint someone else to do them.

29. In your own words, tell the biblical story of humility given in the text.
    _____
    _____
    _____

SENSE OF HUMOR

30. Where does the ability to laugh come from? _____
_____
_____

31. How does humor help a leader? _____
_____
_____

32. Give an example of how humor can be used in leadership. _____
_____
_____
_____
_____
_____

INDIGNATION

33. True or False. A leader must never be angry.

34. Compassion itself is a product of _____ against what hurts
humanity.

PATIENCE AND ENDURANCE

35. What does this quality allow us to do? _____
_____
_____
_____
_____
_____
_____
_____

FELLOWSHIP AND FRIENDSHIP

36. Leaders possess the faculty of what? _____
     _____
     _____
     _____
     _____
     _____

37. Even _____ expressed the value of his friends.

DISCRETION

38. What are two others words for discretion? _____
     _____
     _____
     _____

39. True or False. If you really want to help someone who's hurting, you
     confront them with their sin.

40. Effective leaders always go for the _____ option.

INSPIRATIONAL POWER

41. Inspiration encourages people to keep_____.

42. True character is made in _____ and displayed
     _____.

Assignment:

With each quality dealt with in this chapter, think of one way you can incorporate it into your daily life. As you put each one into action, record the results; how difficult it was it for you; how it made you feel; how the other person responded. After you complete this assignment, keep at it, don't give up!

Group Study:

Briefly research the life of Christ looking for ways He exemplified these qualities in His ministry.

Memory Verse:

Isaiah 42:6 "I, the Lord, have called you in righteousness; I will take hold of your hand. I will keep you and will make you to be a covenant for the people."

CHAPTER 10

THE PRICE OF LEADERSHIP

Scripture: Psalm 32

In this chapter you will learn:

What it takes to be a leader, and whether or not you are willing to do it.

1. True or False. The more effective your leadership, the less you have to worry about sacrifice.

2. What was the formula Jesus gave for great leadership? _____
    _____
    _____
    _____
    _____

PERSONAL SACRIFICE

3. Where do leaders put other's needs in comparison to their own?
    _____
    _____
    _____

4. Is there any way around the cost of personal sacrifice? _____
    _____

5. True leaders have found a purpose and objective to live for and what?
    _____
    _____

REJECTION

6. If you are willing to accept the call to leadership, you must be willing to be
    _____ and _____ by all.

7. How did Jesus pay this price? _____
    _____
    _____
    _____
    _____

8. What does the nature of change bring? _____
    _____
    _____

CRITICISM

9. What does the nature of leadership involve?
    a. taking a position on issues
    b. making decisions
    c. determining direction
    d. all of the above

10. Criticism is usually the manifestation of _____,
    _____ or _____.

11. Is this normal? _____

12. If you are ready for _____, you're ready for
    _____.

LONELINESS

13. True or False. To lead means you must be out in front, ahead of the crowd.

14. A leader must live what at the same time? _____
   _____
   _____
   _____
   _____
   _____

15. Who is the loneliest person today?_____
   _____
   _____
   _____

> **"If you are not willing to stand alone in your vision,**
> **not many will be willing to stand with you."**

PRESSURE AND PERPLEXITY

16. Under what conditions is a leader often called on to make decisions?
   _____
   _____
   _____
   _____
   _____

17. True or False. A Christian leader doesn't have to worry about managing stress.

18. From what resource do we get the information to make good decisions?
   _____
   _____
   _____
   _____
   _____
   _____

MENTAL AND PHYSICAL FATIGUE

19.   What must we be willing to do if we want to be effective leaders?

     _____

     _____

     _____

20.   True or False. Diet and exercise are not important factors in the life of a Christian leader.

21.   How often do you get away in order to restore the soul, mind and body?

     _____

     _____

Remember, it doesn't have to be an expensive vacation to accomplish the purpose of restoration–just quietness and solitude so you can rest and hear the voice of God more clearly.

PRICE PAID BY OTHERS

22.   Whom does leadership demand sacrifice from?_____

     _____

     _____

     _____

23.   Between what must we keep a balance? _____

     _____

     _____

Assignment:

It's time to brainstorm! Under each category presented in this chapter, think of all your fears and worries. Is there an area that is more difficult for you to deal with? Is it harder to take care of yourself, or others? Can you handle rejection and stand on your own? Write all of these things out in your notebook.

Now, think of how God can meet these needs. In your daily devotions, begin searching the Scriptures for God's promises that deal directly with these fears. For example, "I can do all things through Christ which strengtheneth me." Phil. 4:13. Keep a record of your progress and God's provision.

Group Study:

Discuss the principles on page 163. Talk about rejection and criticism, how can it be dealt with? How did Christ deal with it?

Memory Verse:

Psalm 32:8 "I will instruct you and teach you in the way you should go; I will counsel you and watch over you."

CHAPTER 11

THE DANGERS OF LEADERSHIP

Scripture: Ephesians 3:14-21

In this chapter you will learn:

1. The pitfalls of leadership
2. Positive leadership qualities

POPULARITY

1. True or False. A leader must watch that he doesn't encourage the over-estimation of himself so that he becomes the focus of attention.

2. How can you keep this from happening? _____
   _____
   _____
   _____
   _____

3. True leaders do not confuse _____ with
   _____.

PRIDE

4.   Where does pride come from? _____

_____

_____

_____

5.   In your own words, where does our worth come from and how should it
     be measured? _____

_____

_____

_____

_____

6.   How is a sense of superiority maintained? _____

_____

_____

_____

_____

_____

EGOTISM AND INDISPENSABILITY

7.   An egotist considers everything in relation to:
     a. the Bible
     b. himself
     c. others

8.   True or False. The success of everything depends on the leader.

9.   Leaders are only a _____ in a long, historical
     _____.

JEALOUSY

10. How does a true leader NOT measure himself? _____
_____
_____
_____

11. How DOES he measure himself? _____
_____
_____
_____
_____
_____

12. For what will God reward you? _____
_____
_____

DISQUALIFICATION

13. What must a leader be diligent to do? _____
_____
_____

14. Can you effect the change this world needs? _____
_____

15. How? _____
_____
_____
_____
_____
_____

Assignment:

Think of an example of how each danger can manifest itself in the life of a leader. What can you do personally to keep each of these dangers from taking root in your heart. Find a verse of Scripture for each category that you can keep before you at all times.

Group Study:

Find and discuss biblical examples for each category.

Memory Verse:

Ephesians 3:16 "I pray that out of his glorious riches he may strengthen you with power through his Spirit in your inner being."

Leaders learn by leading, because the only real laboratory is the laboratory of leadership itself. Leaders not only manage change, they must be comfortable with it in their own lives. Because we can all change then there is always room for improvement, refinement, cultivation and further development of our skills, character, knowledge and refinement of hidden talents and gifts.

Listed below are principles that must be present and developed if the leader is to deploy and maximize his full potential. Check yourself against the following list and review it as you endeavor to incorporate each principle into your life and leadership.

1. I POSSESS A DEEP GUIDING PURPOSE

You must possess a deep guiding purpose, vision and a sense of destiny for your existence. You must know the significance for your life and have discovered the reason for your existence.

2. I HAVE A CLEAR VISION

You must have a personal and corporate vision. Just as no great painting has ever been created by a committee, no great vision has ever emerged from the head.

3. I LOVE TO SERVE OTHERS

You must live to serve others with a passion to see their lives improve and to maximize their potential.

4. I HAVE ESTABLISHED SPECIFIC GOALS

You must be goal oriented with documented, clearly defined personal and corporate goals that you intend to achieve.

5. I CULTIVATE MY SPIRITUAL RESERVES

You must have an intimate, personal relationship with your Creator and the Lord Jesus Christ. You must reserve regular times for solitude, prayer and meditation to replenish spiritual reserves.

6. I AM TEACHABLE

You must operate on the assumption that, all I know is what I have learned and all I have learned is not all there is to know.

7. I AM CONSTANTLY REFINING MY SKILLS

You must constantly develop and refine your skills through an ongoing program of study–understanding that mastery and absolute competence is mandatory for a leader.

8. I AM TOLERANT

You must be patient, allowing others to fail and grow, understanding that potential is more valuable than behavior.

9. I AM HONEST AND SINCERE WITH INTEGRITY

You must maintain the highest standard of integrity, honestly integrating your words, feelings, actions and thoughts into one complete whole.

10. I COMMUNICATE MY VISION

You must communicate your vision, what is to be done, who is to do it, and how it is to be done.

11. I AM AN AVID READER

You must read widely and deeply to cultivate the habit of sharpening your knowledge base. I keep up with current issues by reading the best literature, magazines, books, journals, etc.

12. I MAXIMIZE TIME

You must be deeply sensitive to the value of time and be meticulously careful in your selection of priorities.

13. I AM ENTHUSIASTIC TOWARD LIFE

You must radiate positive energy with an optimistic attitude and an enthusiastic spirit, full of hope and faith.

14. I BELIEVE IN THE WORTH AND VALUE OF OTHERS

You must believe in other people and appreciate their value and potential.

15. I KEEP MYSELF IN THE BEST CONDITION POSSIBLE

You must maintain a balanced, moderate, regular program of exercise and proper diet to enhance your physical, mental, emotional and spiritual well being.

16. I EMBRACE RESPONSIBILITY CHEERFULLY

You must avoid procrastination and embrace active responsibility.

17. I AM DARING

You must initiate new ventures and welcome new ideas without fear of challenging convention and tradition.

18. I AM DECISIVE

You must make decisions and be fully aware of and accept the consequences of your decisions.

19. I AM RESULT ORIENTED

You must care more for the accomplishment of the task than who gets the credit.

20. I AM COMMITTED TO EXCELLENCE

You must give more than is expected of you and take pride in every task.

21. I LEARN FROM MY MISTAKES

You must learn from your mistakes and failures rather than allowing them to discourage, defeat or immobilize you.

22. I MEASURE MYSELF AGAINST MYSELF

You must measure your performance and success only against your potential and your purpose without comparing yourself or achievements to other people.

NOTE: "If you would be successful as a leader, discover what people want and help them achieve it." Your success comes when you are helping other people achieve what is important to them.

EXERCISE: Complete the following assignment as a personal commitment to enhancing your leadership edge: Take a blank sheet of paper and write your personal response.

My Purpose   –   Why I exist

My Vision   –   Where I intend to go

My Goals   –   What I intend to go

My Objectives   –   How I intend to do it

My Plan   –   Procedure

My Strategy   –   Co-ordination of Resources

After you have completed this exercise, read this book again and commit to deploy the great leader within you.

I AM A LEADER

1.   I POSSESS A DEEP GUIDING PURPOSE

2.   I HAVE A CLEAR VISION

3.   I LOVE TO SERVE OTHERS

4.   I HAVE ESTABLISHED SPECIFIC GOALS

5.   I CULTIVATE MY SPIRITUAL RESERVES

6.   I AM TEACHABLE

7.   I AM CONSTANTLY REFINING MY SKILLS

8.   I AM TOLERANT

9.   I AM HONEST AND SINCERE WITH INTEGRITY

10.   I COMMUNICATE MY VISION

11.   I AM AN AVID READER

12.   I MAXIMIZE TIME

13.   I AM ENTHUSIASTIC TOWARD LIFE

14. I BELIEVE IN THE WORTH AND VALUE OTHERS

15. I KEEP MYSELF IN THE BEST CONDITION POSSIBLE

16. I EMBRACE RESPONSIBILITY CAREFULLY

17. I AM DARING

18. I AM DECISIVE

19. I AM RESULT ORIENTED

20. I AM COMMITTED TO EXCELLENCE

21. I LEARN FROM MY MISTAKES

22. I MEASURE MYSELF AGAINST MYSELF

"Be a leader, led by the Great Leader of leaders, Jesus Christ!"

ANSWER KEY - CHAPTER ONE

1. The ability to lead others by influence.
2. Your own answer.
3. what you do, becoming who you are.
4. One is born to lead, while others are born to follow and be subordinate.
5. No.
6. character, vision
7. a. Moses - lawgiver
   b. Gideon - deliverer of his nation
   c. David - King of Israel
   d. Peter - leader of the Christian church.
8. a. Fugitive from Pharoh's justice and a murder
   b. Cowardice
   c. insignificance
   d. a simple fisherman.
9. Your own answer.
10. Yes.
11. b.
12. When you discover the purpose and vision for your life, and set out to fulfill it without compromise.
13. Your own answer.
14. In His image and likeness.
15. Spirit of rulership, authority.
16. a. God created man to have dominion over the earth.
    b. God gave dominion over the earth to both male and female.
    c. He never gave man the authority to dominate one another.
    d. He specified what they were to dominate "...the earth and creation."
    e. They were created to dominate and not be dominated.
17. c.
18. The removal of the Spirit of God from man's spirit.
19. To restore his Holy Spirit back to man and thus restore self-government.
20. The Holy Spirit.

ANSWER KEY - CHAPTER TWO
1. Yes.
2. designated position, individual
3. function, position, exercise, responsibility

4. Your own answer.

5. No.

6. Your own answer.

7. The correct words are:

influence, inspiration, momentum, motivation, mobilize, confidence.

8. d.

9. Your own answer.

10. Your own answer.

11. c.

12. A passion for accomplishment.

13.   a. values

      b. deep convictions

      c. correct principles

14. revelation, restraint.

15.   a. vision and values

      b. inspiring and motivating others to work together with a common purpose.

16. c.

17. influence through inspiration.

18. intimidation, manipulation.

19. Your own answer.

ANSWER KEY - CHAPTER THREE

1. T

2. born, become

3. c.

4. Your own answer.

5. F

6. Your own answer.

7. a. purpose

   b. passion

   c. integrity

   d. trust

   e. curiosity and daring

8. reason, meaning

9. Your own answer.

10. Your own answer.

11. d.

12. self-knowledge, candor, maturity.

13. T

14. Your own answer.
15. acquired, earned.
16. time, integrity.
17. Your own answer.
18. risks, faith, try, challenge
19. Yes
20. A strong sense of purpose.
21. F
22. Who you are and who you want to be from what the world thinks you are and wants you to be.
23. Express themselves.
24. Your own answer.
25.   a. Those who make things happen.
     b. Those who watch things happen.
     c. Those who let things happen.
     d. Those who ask "What happened?"
26. a.
27. master, surrender
28. T
29. Make everyone else over in his own image.
30. F

ANSWER KEY - CHAPTER FOUR

1. b.
2. not doing things right, but doing the right thing.
3. wrong, fail.
4. effective, progressive.
5. purpose.
6. a.
7. How followers were created and the objective for following.
8. provides
9. Yes.
10. He disobeyed God's laws.
11. F
12. discovering, become
13. b.
14.   a. dependence
     b. independence
     c. interdependence

15. One of the examples listed on
16. When you have discovered yourself and your unique purpose.
17. to inspire every follower to become a leader.
18. Your own answer.
19. a.
20. successor
21. Your own answer.

Assignment:
1. apostles, prophets,evangelists, pastors & teachers.
2. to prepare (train) God's people for the works of service (leadership)
3. A. so that the Body of Christ may be built up
    B. until we all reach unity in the faith and knowledge of the Son of God
    C. and become mature (responsible, independent)
    D. attaining to the whole measure of the fullness of Christ.
4. Then we will no longer be infants . . .

ANSWER KEY - CHAPTER FIVE

1. d.
2. Three of the following:
    "Am I willing to serve?"
    "Am I willing to be patient?"
    "Am I willing to say, 'I'm available?'"
    "Am I prepared for the cost and price of leadership?"
3. a.
4. experience.
5. T
6. F
7. prepared.
8. From its motivation.
9. Greed and lust for power.
10. Your own answer.
11. F
12. When it comes from a desire to serve.
13. F
14. selfless service.
15. c.
16. Your own answer.

17. The nature of God and the welfare of others.
18. Personal sacrifice for the sake of others.
19. Your own answer.

ANSWER KEY - CHAPTER SIX

1. a. resistance
   b. resignation
   c. submission
2. Push back.
3. Try to get away from it.
4. Make little or no effort to think or contribute to the organization.
5. Your own answer.
6. Three of the following:
      fear, intimidation, obligation, dependency, guilt
7. F
8. a.
9. d.
10. God, Himself.
11. b.
12. You become free from the opinions of men.
13. One
14. You must return to the manufacturer for his original plan for your life.
15. F
16. little, bigger
17. Leads, not by merely pointing the way, but by having trodden it himself.
18. F
19. ambition, serve
20. c.
21. Abuse and self-destruction result.
22. Three from the list on.
23. T
24. Because of his dependence on God.

ANSWER KEY - CHAPTER SEVEN PART ONE

1. d.
2. F
3. raw material.
4. Your own answer.

5. learn, made
6. John 7:1-6 or any other that applies.
7. Your own answer.
8. b.
9. Your own answer.
10. Your own answer.
11. F
12. wise, temper.
13. Your own answer.
14. F
15. weigh, all
16. Your own answer.
17. a.
18. Your own answer.
19. opportunities, potential, surprise.
20. Jesus, Paul and Moses.
21. Your own answer.
22. Your own answer.
23. a. Your faithfulness in little things.
     b. Commitment to your purpose.
     c. Willingness to die for your cause.
24. Your own answer.
25. Daniel
26. Your own answer.
27. If others reprimand themselves when they disappoint you.
28. Your own answer.
29. inspiration.
30. Your own answer.
31. the ability to discover common ground between opposing viewpoints and then induce both parties to accept it.
32. Your own answer.
33. Your own answer.
34. "The brother offended is harder to win than a city with walls."
35. Your own answer.
36. help, like
37. Your own answer.
38. Before kings.
39. Your own answer.

40. Your own answer.
41. Your own answer.
42. Aaron

ANSWER KEY - CHAPTER SEVEN PART TWO

1. Your own answer.
2. Answers from list on.
3. F
4. Your own answer.
5. Your own answer.
6. Jesus
7. Your own answer.
8. F
9. He corrects them and tries to help them learn their lessons so they can do it better the next time.
10. F

ANSWER KEY - CHAPTER EIGHT

1. Competence, vision, and virtue.
2. F
3. b.
4. born, life.
5. A commitment to the qualifications presented in this chapter.
6. F
7. I Timothy 3:1-7
8. In marriage.
9. talented, faithful.
10. F
11. By not allowing himself to carry secrets that could undermine his character or mar his public witness.
12. Wait a while before he allows himself to be used.
13. quick, slow, angry.
14. estimation, Jesus Christ.
15. Garbage
16. a.
17. manipulated
18. b.
19. control, wise

20. The ability to accept the differences in others' opinions, views, personalities, characters, positions and status without being threatened in your own security.
21. a.
22. time, qualify, trust
23. c.
24. teach, learn.
25. F
26. Four things from the list on.
27. initiate
28. b.
29. stewardship.
30. Those he is leading and his personal resources.
31. energies, resources and materials

ANSWER KEY - CHAPTER NINE

1. decision.
2. T
3. The self-disciplined.
4. Someone who could see beyond what everybody else was looking at.
5. insight.
6. F
7. perish.
8. drudgery.
9. Discipline and self-motivation.
10. Your own answer.
11. Wisdom
12. the ability to use knowledge effectively.
13. Three of the following: judgment, discernment, comprehension, insight, hindsight, foresight
14. education.
15. c.
16. decision.
17. yes, no
18. b.
19. Moral
20. Firmness
21. F
22. c.

23. a.
24. naturally
25. Your own answer.
26. T
27. b.
28. F
29. Your own answer.
30. Our Creator.
31. In maintaining a proper perspective in life.
32. To transform a tense situation into a positive one. Or, your own answer.
33. F
34. anger
35. To make room for others to fail and be different.
36. Being able to attract and draw the best out of other people.
37. Jesus
38. Tact and diplomacy.
39. F
40. win/win
41. moving.
42. secret, openly.

ANSWER KEY - CHAPTER TEN

1. F
2. Whoever wants to become great among you must be your servant, and whoever wants to be first must be slave of all.
3. Above themselves.
4. No
5. A vision to die for.
6. rejected, misunderstood
7. When he was rejected by his own community.
8. Conflict and resistance.
9. d.
10. jealousy, insecurity or fear.
11. Yes
12. criticism, leadership.
13. T
14. Both the process and destination.
15. The one who has been entrusted with a vision that is ahead of his time.

16. Under time constraints and external pressure.
17. F
18. Experience and knowledge of the Word.
19. Be willing to work harder, more intense, and beyond the call of duty.
20. F
21. Your own answer.
22. The leader, their spouse, children, family and close friends.
23. Between serving the people and meeting our family's needs.

ANSWER KEY - CHAPTER ELEVEN
1. T
2. By focusing the attention of the people on the Lord Jesus Christ and His vision to which you are called.
3. applause, affirmation.
4. From believing the praise of men as the true measure of your worth.
5. Your own answer.
6. By the maintenance of the feeling of inferiority in others.
7. b.
8. F
9. link, chain.
10. In comparison to others.
11. By his own purpose and vision.
12. For obedience to your own vision.
13. Guard his heart, mind and life from any compromise.
14. Yes
15. By rising up and allowing God to train you for leadership.

Other Books By Myles Munroe

The Principle of Fatherhood
Priority, Position, and the Role of the Male
by Myles Munroe

With clarity, logic, and love, Dr. Munroe insightfully demonstrates his point that the inherent purpose within all men is fatherhood, and that fatherhood carries the tantamount principles of leadership, integrity, responsibility, and obedience to the Father of all fathers. With these principles in place, true fathers come to understand that their true identity is gleaned from God, and that their main responsibility as fathers is to lead their families to fellowship. This book is a complete, yet succinct guide for fathers—and fathers-in-training—to measure their effectiveness in our modern society.

Seasons of Change
Understanding Purpose In Times Of Perplexity
by Myles Munroe

In this landmark work, Dr. Myles Munroe draws plans for the transformation of our society during the coming economic, political, social and cultural changes. Dr. Munroe reveals how to unlock ourselves from the prison of our present circumstances, and experience security, confidence and freedom in the uncertainty of our changing world.

We must prepare ourselves for the inevitable changes we all must face. Dr. Munroe shows us that we must "rethink" our approaches and be willing to embrace new attitudes in ever-increasingly fresh ways. *Seasons of Change* demonstrates that the renewal of our nation and our world will not come from our present social and political system as it exists right now; it will come from deep within us.

Myles Munroe on Leadership
Inspirational Quotes for the Frontline Leader
by Myles Munroe

This book will give you a whole new perspective on what it means to become an effective leader. This book is a gallery of superb ideas on leadership and how it relates to influence, self-mastery, determination, courage, criticism and countless other eye-opening ideas.

Myles Munroe On Leadership will reveal to you infinite possibilities for reaching your full leadership potential. Rediscover your hidden talents for leadership at the highest level possible. Here are the answers you have always wanted. Dr. Munroe takes the mystery out of leadership by unlocking the secrets of over 150 enlightening new insights.

Singles 101
Keys to Wholeness and Fulfillment
by Myles Munroe

Being single does not mean being lonely!
Author and teacher Myles Munroe captures the essence of living the single life in 101 poignant, encouraging quips and quotes. Munroe believes that if you are single, you have the unique and rare opportunity to discover what it means to be separate, unique, and whole and that being alone does not mean being lonely. Absorb Munroe's spiritual and practical advice for a quick lift to get you through the day, or for more profound contemplation during your prayer and devotional times. Either way, you will discover the joy of being single.

Sex 101
Unlocking Hidden Truths About Sex
by Myles Munroe & David Burrows

Whether you are a teenager or an adult, *Sex 101* is your survival manual. This book will guide as well as protect you against the barrage of incorrect attitudes and ideas by revealing hidden truths about sex. This timely, monumental book will unlock the shackles of defrauded and enticing words and images that you may have been exposed to. After reading this handy book, you will make key distinctions that will help you control and conquer situations that may have caused you to compromise in the past or in the future. *Sex 101* will help you set a higher standard for yourself and those around you.

Marriage 101
Building a Healthy Relationship with Your Mate
by Dr. Myles Munroe

Marriage is God's idea. And it can be one of the best things a man and woman will ever experience—if they fully dedicate their life together to God. This powerful little book provides just the right ingredients to help married couples achieve that glorious oneness that God intended for them. In it, you'll find a wealth of material on such subjects as keeping live alive, mutual submission, fidelity and the power of forgiveness. Filled with on-target insights and practical help, *Marriage 101* is ideal for young couples just starting out—or for any marriage that could use a recharge, or even a jump-start.

Videos By Myles Munroe

The Church 2000   2 Video Tapes
Leading in the New Millennium
by Dr. Myles Munroe

This eye-opening video reveals how to adapt to life in the new millennium. Dr. Munroe has traveled around the world, meeting with corporate, church, and governmental leaders to find the secrets to taking charge in the year 2000. In simple, yet profound terms, he describes what he had learned and gives to you four keys to reaching your potential: wisdom, relevance, skill, and diplomacy.

Like a surgeon's scalpel, Dr. Munroe cuts through much of the spiritual nonsense that plagues many christians. He illustrates how you can lead the way to making a lasting change in yourself, and in the church. God is looking for a new kind of leader.

Becoming A Leader   Video
Everyone Can Do It
by Dr. Myles Munroe

This video has been used by Fortune 500 corporations, universities, and international leaders as a tool for leadership development. It uncovers the secrets of dynamic leadership that will turn your leadership potential into a potent reality. To become a front runner, you must successfully overcome barriers to your effectiveness as a leader. You will be encouraged, provoked and stimulated as "leadership power" is literally activated within you through this video.

The Golden Keys To Fulfilling Your Vision   **Video**
How to Transform Your Dreams Into Reality
by Myles Munroe

The Golden Keys To Fulfilling Your Vision will make you feel a strong, gripping enthusiasm to take immediate action to advance your vision. Myles Munroe shows you exactly how to access your dreams in the deepest, most fulfilling and practical way possible. This video will motivate you to start planning your vision more rapidly than anything else you will ever see or hear.

In Pursuit of Purpose   **Video**
Discovering the Key to Personal Fulfillment
by Myles Munroe

Fulfillment in life is dependent on your becoming and doing what you were born to be and do. For without purpose, life has no reason. Join Dr. Munroe for a journey in the pursuit of your purpose and destiny. On this journey of pursuing purpose, ask yourself some searching questions, challenge your resolve, check you definitions of life, evaluate your past success and create your strategy to accomplish everything that you were born to achieve.

The Hidden Glory   **Video**
Uncovering the Treasure Within
by Myles Munroe

Do you wonder who you are today? Are you certain of the person you have become in recent years? This video is about the process of discovery... it's about becoming who you were born to be. Are you ready to be introduced to yourself, perhaps for the first time?

Never judge yourself by your present state because you are still being unwrapped. "Each stage of your life is only a layer. God will peel away each layer to reveal your true self." Take care not to throw away the precious, hidden glory buried deep within you before it has come to the surface. This video will help you to meet the real you and teach you how to live a full, expressive life. Don't you dare die without ever having lived.

Single, Married, Separated & Life After Divorce   Video
by Myles Munroe

In this video, Dr. Munroe explains the importance of being a "single, separate, unique and whole" person in Christ before marriage; the importance of being joined together in Christ in marriage; and the very serious issues of separation and divorce. He clearly explains what the Bible has to say about relationships. Dr. Munroe also shares on other issues:

- How do I know when I am ready for marriage?
- What about remarriage?
- What do you do with the hurt?
- How do you forgive?

Whether you are single, married, separated or divorced, Dr. Munroe's practical and insightful advice will guide you in making some of life's most important decisions.

Maximizing Your Singleness   Video
Embracing Wholeness and Completion
by Myles Munroe

All your life you may have been programmed by your environment to believe that being "single" and "unmarried" were the same—that "unmarried" means "incomplete." Embracing your singleness means you are unique and whole. Knowing that you are like no one else gives you a wholeness that you can share with someone else. Unmarried doesn't mean you are single... just unmarried. Marriage is a choice, not a necessity for completion. Knowing that you are your best investment as a whole, single person frees you to give yourself the gift of personal development and refinement and encourage others to become whole in their singleness.

Understanding Your Potential   Video
Discovering the Hidden You
by Myles Munroe

Understanding Your Potential is an inspiring look into the abundant potential locked inside of you that is waiting to be discovered and activated. This video will provoke you to become uneasy with your past achievements, motivate you to set your goals and fulfill your destiny.

Maximizing Your Potential   Video
The Keys to Dying Empty
by Myles Munroe

The greatest threat to being all you could be is satisfaction with who you are. What you could do is always endangered by what you have done.

This video is for the individual who knows that somewhere deep inside, there is still so much you have not released: so much yet to do, so much left to expose. Myles Munroe teaches you how to experience what he calls maximum living: beyond doing good to experiencing your best. Learn to die empty. Die fulfilled by dying unfilled, not prematurely.

The Kingdom of Ignorant Kings   **Video**
Discovering Your Inheritance
by Myles Munroe

Dr. Munroe dispels the myths and misunderstandings we have about God's Kingdom by applying spiritual principles that empower you to reclaim the "old" position from which mankind has fallen. You will begin to live day-by-day in the "Kingdom of Re-Educated Kings." This is the Kingdom Jesus talked about. This kingdom is filled with health and prosperity. In this kingdom your whole life is filled with peace and you live without fear or depression. Salvation is the doorway and the Kingdom is "what's inside". Dr. Munroe shows you how to step inside.

Books by Other Authors of Pneuma Life Publishng

Eternal Victim / Eternal Victor
by Donnie McClurkin

Through the guilt, the pains, the fears, and the loss, there is forgiveness, there is healing, there is restoration of confidence and joy, there is great gain . . . there is an eternal victor!

Remembering and recounting the ordeals of his early childhood, Donnie McClurkin resurrects feelings of hurt and pain that had long been forgotten. He causes himself to reveal the scars of healed wounds, explain how it happened, how he endured, and how he and his family came out delivered and victorious. This truly personal testimony by one of Gospel music's favorite artists, shares his tremendous compassion for those who have not received healing for their hurts, as well as those who are still in the midst of their personal struggles–especially the children.

From the moment he neglected watching his two-year old brother, only to see him toddle into the street and be tragically killed by a speeding car, to the extreme sexual violation of an uncle who took advantage of his childhood innocence, to his bout with homosexuality, McClurkin candidly recounts the steps he took to turn his life from a victim to a victor.

"Victims and victors have one thing in common," says McClurkin, "–suffering. They both encounter conflict, contest and combat. Each endures hurt, heartache, and hell. Abuse and failure, broken dreams, and bouts with identity are commonplace. But it is how one handles those events that classifies whether they are one or the other."

My friend, you are not alone. Your situation is not unique, but your victorious end is assured if you journey the road to victory! Remember, everything that was said about you in the past, negatively, is of no consequence. Regardless of all your mistakes and faults, you are not a failure! Have a change of heart, change of mind, and even a change in your speech and declare that failure is not an option. Proclaim victory over those past ordeals!

Wife 101
Everything Your Husband wished You Already Knew

Wife 101 gives you two hundred incredible ways to create a more exciting and meaningful relationship. You will gain a new sense of confidence by understanding the things your husband needs from you to function in harmony with you. When you read and apply the *Wife 101* principles, you will begin to implement the key elements your spouse needs to experience total happiness, complete fulfillment and enrichment. You will understand how to communicate with the language of his heart. Ignite the spark of burning love in your relationship all over again… and discover how to keep it fresh.

Wife 101 will teach you how to rekindle the feelings you first shared with your husband. It is a mini-course in how to experience life's most treasured moments with him. *Wife 101* will give you endless streams of new insights about your marriage from your husband's perspective.

Husband 101
Everything Your Wife Wished You Already Knew

Husband 101 is a step-by-step mini-course in how to begin an engaging new love affair with your wife. When you apply these simple ideas, your wife will connect with you at a much higher level. By taking every action in this book, you will automatically build a bridge to your wife's heart. She will begin to understand you dynamically because you will learn to speak the language of her heart–maybe for the first time. She will instantly begin to respond to you in exciting and meaningful new ways.

Husband 101 will give your marriage the "booster shot" you've been looking for. This book will show you how to recapture the flame of your wife's passion for you again and again. *Husband 101* is a step-by-step mini-course on how to begin an engaging new love affair with your wife.

Weight Loss 101

Overwhelmed by useless diets often doing more harm than good? *Weight Loss 101* is a refreshing key to unlocking the door to a healthier you. In a market inundated by empty promises, vain dreams, popular fads, and deceptive schemes, *Weight Loss 101* provides you with effective and innovative ways to finally attaining your ideal weight and health goals.

With over 150 time-tested tips and proven methods, *Weight Loss 101* is a step-by-step guide that will undoubtedly help you triumph in your war against unwanted weight. As your personal trainer, *Weight Loss 101* will coach you to your success and motivate you to achieving a higher and healthier standard of living-one step at a time.

True Worship Experience
by Eric Kwapong

Eric demonstrates how true worship is based upon giving God our total love-a love so strong, so pure, so heart and Spirit-felt that it actually touches Him. This is the type of worship God craves, expects, and deserves, and this type of worship is what will fulfill you in return. With Biblical examples and helpful tips.

The Church
A Mystery Revealed
by Turnel Nelson

God's purpose and intent for the Church is that it be an international embassy on earth that manifests the policies, dictates and purposes of the Kingdom of God. This book outlines some of the fundamental measures that need to be taken in order to revitalize the Church for 21st century evangelism and discipleship.

No More Sheets
The Truth About Sex
by Juanita Bynum

People of faith often forget that we are not on a playground but a battleground. God told us to prepare for warfare. Entrenched in the very idea of war is the understanding that there will be some wounds. This is a very important lesson: We must learn to survive the wounds. Juanita Bynum understands the scars that come in the heat of battle. Over the years, God has shown Juanita how to rid herself of layers of "sheets" (bondage) that had affected her work for God. It was a painful process. She learned the hard way, but you don't have to. You can hasten the healing in your own life by gleaning from Juanita Bynum's experience.

No More Sheets offers hope. More importantly, it offers some answers that can set you free. After reading this book, there are no more excuses! If you want to enjoy the fullness of God, you must cast off those sheets. You must make a declaration for every future relationship: *No More Sheets!*

"Juanita Bynum's clear message of sexual morality is one that is needed for those who have not always had someone to talk frankly about such an issue. She removes the deep shame surrounding the issue by openly discussing her own path to victory. I believe that any of us who work with hurting people can use her strong witness as a reference for counseling as well as a clarion call to prayer and holiness for those of us called to the front lines." - T. D. Jakes

The Morning Glory Series
by Juanita Bynum

The Morning Glory Series will help you put your faith into action. These devotional, prayer, and meditation guides will help you seek and find God in fresh new ways, daily. You will discover refreshingly different applications each time you open the pages of these books.

In this series, Prophetess Bynum reminds us that the morning watch is essential. Each day possesses its own challenge. You must not face the day until you have faced God, nor look into the face of others until you have looked into His. *Morning Glory* will help you in this quest.

The highly anticipated *Devotional* is personal. In it, Prophetess Bynum imparts some of her wisdom, faith, and insight to inspire you to build and achieve admirable qualities such as character, integrity, and discipline. You will be drawn into marvelous places in which your mind will be awakened to envision new truths and grasp wonderful spiritual nuggets.

Meditation Scriptures will help you to find the exact Scripture you need–when you need it most. It contains Prophetess Bynum's favorite Scriptures on those topics critical in the quest to know God and His Word more intimately.

The *Gift Book* capsulizes the truths in each of the *Morning Glory* books. You can use it daily or give it to anyone seeking to know and understand a greater intimacy with God. After studying the other 3 books, you can write down your prayer requests, insights and answers from God in the *Prayer Journal*.

- **Morning Glory Devotional**
- **Morning Glory Meditation Scriptures**
- **Morning Glory Gift Book**
- **Morning Glory Prayer Journal**

Strategies for Saving the Next Generation
by Dave Burrows

This book will teach you how to start and effectively operate a vibrant youth ministry. This book is filled with practical tips and insight gained over a number of years working with young people from the street to the parks to the church. Dave Burrows offers the reader vital information that will produce results if carefully considered and adapted. Excellent for Pastors and Youth Pastor as well as youth workers and those involved with youth ministry.

Sex & Dating
A Guide to Relationships for Teens and Young Adults
by Dave Burrows

Most teenagers live for today. Living only for today, however, can kill you. When teenagers have no plan for their future, they follow a plan that someone else devised. Unfortunately, this plan often leads them to drugs, sex, crime, jail, and an early death. Planning separates winners from losers. Don't be a loser. You can get a plan for your life, develop your skill, achieve your dreams, and still have fun.

The Call of God
by Jefferson Edwards

Since I have been called to preach, Now What? Many sincere Christians are confused about their call to the ministry. Some are zealous and run ahead of their time and season of training and preparation while others are behind their time neglecting the gift of God within them. *The Call of God* gives practical instruction for pastors and leaders to refine and further develop their ministry and tips on how to nourish and develop others with God's Call to effectively proclaim the gospel of Christ.

> *The Call of God* **will help you to:**
> • Have clarity from God as to what ministry involves
> • Be able to identify and affirm the call in your life
> • See what stage you are in your call from God
> • Remove confusion in relation to the processing of a call or the making of the person
> • Understand the development of the anointing to fulfill your call.

Come, Let Us Pray
by Emmette Weir

Are you satisfied with your prayer Life? Are you finding that your prayers are often dull, repetitive and lacking in spiritual power? Are you looking for ways to improve your relationship with God? Would you like to be able to pray more effectively? Then *Come, Let Us Pray* will help you in these areas and more. If you want to gain the maximum spiritual experience from your prayer life and enter into the very presence of God. *Come, Let Us Pray.*

Redeemed & Justified
by Richard Pinder

This book will help you experience the complete gift of righteousness that Jesus has given you. Experience the joy and freedom of understanding Christ's finished work for you. Once a slave in the marketplace of sin, you will feel Jesus break the shackles from your life forever.

Mobilizing Human Resources
by Pastor Richard Pinder

Pastor Pinder gives an in-depth look at how to organize, motivate and deploy members of the body of Christ in a manner that produces maximum effect for your ministry. This book will assist you in organizing and motivating your 'troops' for effective and efficient ministry. It will also help the individual believer in recognizing their place in the body, using their God given abilities and talents to maximum effect.

Leadership in the New Testament Church
by Earl D. Johnson

Leadership in the New Testament Church offers practical and applicable insight into the role of leadership in the present day church. In this book, the author explains the qualities that leaders must have, explores the interpersonal relationships between the leader and his staff, the leaders' influence in the church and society and how to handle conflicts that arise among leaders.

The Minister's Topical Bible
by Derwin Stewart

The Minister's Topical Bible covers every aspect of the ministry providing quick and easy access to scriptures in a variety of ministry related topics. This handy reference tool can be effectively used in leadership training, counseling, teaching, sermon preparation and personal study.

Here at last is practical help for the busy minister. *The Minister's Topical Bible* is the ideal tool for all who could use a little assistance in teaching, preaching and counseling. As an aid in sermon preparation, *The Minister's Topical Bible* is unsurpassed. By collecting all Scripture on a topic in a single place, valuable time is saved from having to search through concordances or trying to bring up passages from memory. A topical approach to the Bible helps ministers gain a fuller picture of the wonderful provision God has made for His people in all areas of life. Additionally, in a step-by-step fashion *The Minister's Topical Bible* covers key areas of ministry including personal life, ministry ethics, discipling, teaching, and preaching in 540 topics. All things considered, *The Minister's Topical Bible* is the most thorough and complete compilation of Bible Scriptures that no minister should be without.
Bonus: Also contains "What is Leadership?" by Myles Munroe

Printed in the United States
6507